To Charlie, James, + Thomas Hale,

I pray you will love God with all your heart. And I pray you will love this country He's blessed us to live in.

♡ Sarah White

The Land of Red, White, and Blue

ISBN 978-1-68570-083-6 (paperback)
ISBN 978-1-68570-323-3 (hardcover)
ISBN 978-1-68570-084-3 (digital)

Christian Faith Publishing
832 Park Avenue
Meadville, PA 16335
www.christianfaithpublishing.com

Printed in the United States of America

The Land of Red, White, and Blue

SARAH WHITE

You live in the land of red, white, and blue,
Where many brave men and women have died for you.
They gave up their lives for you and for me,
So that we could live in a land that is free.

There are many holidays throughout the year,
To show these special people that they are revered.
To *revere* means to show lots of respect and admiration,
And who more deserving than soldiers of this great nation?

These American soldiers have served us in such a great way,
And serving is something you and I can do every single day!
To *serve* is to do something good for someone else,
So let's think of ways we can serve someone other than ourself!

Don't you want to follow the example of our heroes?
When we serve other people, our love for them shows.
Serving is also a way to say that we're thankful to the Lord.
What are some things you're thankful for?

God created each of us to be unique and to love Him,
Did you know that God's love for us never ends?
The people who founded America knew this,
So they wrote a Constitution for all of us.

The Constitution was written hundreds of years ago,
And it's just as important today as it was when they wrote
"We the People." "The People" is us—it's you and me,
And we the people have liberty.

Liberty is a gift that not everyone in the world gets to enjoy,
Liberty means freedom—freedom for every girl and boy.
We are free to go to school and learn, to come home and play,
We are free to say what we think, go to church, and pray.

We are so very blessed to live in this place,
For many people in other countries, that is not the case.
So let's give thanks to God each and every day,
For His love, for America and its heroes, and for the life we have today.

Pray for Our Heroes

Dear Lord,

Thank You for blessing us to live in this nation where we are free. Let us never forget the price that has been paid for our freedom. May we live with thankfulness to You and to our heroes. And may we follow their example to love and serve others every day. And most of all, thank You for sending Your Son, Jesus, to die for us so that we could be free forever and have eternal life with You.

Amen.

Give to Our Heroes

Not only can we read about, talk about, and pray for our heroes but also we can support them by donating money to meet their needs! Check out organizations like the Wounded Warrior Project, Tunnel to Towers, Operation First Response, Children of Fallen Patriots Foundation, and so many more.

The challenge here is that as a family, you would partner together with one or more of these organizations to support our heroes and truly thank them for their service by donating. They have blessed us; let's bless them back!

About the Author

Sarah was born and raised in South Louisiana, where she has chosen to stay. A lover of theology, politics, and analyzing culture, she's always been a thinker and writer at heart.

This is her first children's book in a series of works aiming to inspire young families to stand upon the truth of Scripture in a world set against it.

As she recently welcomed her first nephew into the world, her passion for the next generation has only intensified. She hopes to use whatever talents and resources the Lord has given her to be a beacon of truth and hope to whoever has ears to hear and an encouragement to those who have hearts to do the same.

She is proud to live in this country God has blessed so much and has the desire for all to know that one true God. She hopes this book will be a small tool in that effort to inspire young kids and their families to love their country and, together, pray for and give to those who've fought to protect it. And most of all, she hopes every reader will know God and love Him.